84 CHARING CROSS ROAD

84 Charing Cross Road

by HELENE HANFF

Adapted for the Stage
by JAMES ROOSE-EVANS

NELSON DOUBLEDAY, INC. GARDEN CITY, NEW YORK

84 CHARING CROSS ROAD began its American run on December 14, 1982 at the Nederlander Theatre in New York City. The production was directed by James Roose-Evans; scenery by Oliver Smith; lighting by Marc B. Weiss; costumes by Pearl Somner. The cast was as follows:

HELENE HANFF	*Ellen Burstyn*
FRANK DOEL	*Joseph Maher*
CECILY FARR	*Ellen Newman*
MEGAN WELLS	*Jo Henderson*
GEORGE MARTIN	*William Francis*
WILLIAM HUMPHRIES	*Mark Chamberlin*
MAXINE STUART	*Jo Henderson*
JOAN TODD	*Etain O'Malley*
THOMAS	*Thomas Nahrwold*

The action of the play is set in the New York apartment of Helene Hanff and in the bookshop of Marks & Co., 84 Charing Cross Road, London. The action spans the years 1949-71.

ACT ONE

ACT ONE

The set is the shop and it covers the entire stage. When the curtain rises we glimpse only Helene Hanff's apartment, however, where she is seated at her desk working, smoke curling up from her cigarette. The floor in front of the desk, by the wastepaper basket, is littered with screwed-up balls of typing paper—discarded efforts. Later, Helene Hanff will tidy these up. Her apartment is cluttered, and with evidence of orange-crate bookshelves, and a board for pinning up cards, mementos, and cuttings. Soon light will shaft through the windows of the shop and the first person we shall see is Frank Doel standing at his desk, H.H.'s first letter in his hand. As more lights come up we shall discover Cecily Farr standing on a stepladder looking for a book, and Megan Wells seated at an upstage table, checking accounts. A little later Mr. George Martin enters to check a query with Megan, then with Cecily. Finally Megan rings a small handbell and there enters Bill Humphries.

Through the windows of the shop—books displayed on the shelves—we can glimpse the street outside. A sign which reads CLOSED *on one side and* OPEN *on the other hangs at the glass-paneled door of the shop, and there are the usual prints clipped to a string across the door.*

Helene's room must be differentiated from the shop on a higher level, yet in style a recognizable part of the shop. In reality she lives in New York but, increasingly, during the play, she comes to live in the shop in her imagination.

At no time does the actress playing Helene Hanff have eye contact with the other actors or they with her. The occupants of the shop act in a naturalistic style when interacting among themselves, but when in communication with Helene they must be acutely aware of her, and she of them, but never looking directly at each other. At the very first meeting of Rosemary Leach and David Swift, who created the roles on stage, I had them read the play with their backs to each other, thus establishing from the start that heightened awareness of two people who never meet and yet come close to each other.

There are books everywhere, all over the floor, as well as on the shelves. There are mounds of catalogs, old torn books, ephemera of all kinds. The table center stage is set aside for especially rare old books which are handled with care. Most of the stock will be leather-bound and of quality.

With the cue for houselights, we hear the opening section of Gershwin's "Rhapsody in Blue." The curtain rises and we see H.H. consulting the Saturday Review of Literature, *a cigarette in her mouth. She removes the cigarette, puts down the* Review, *and begins to type. At a climax in the music she pulls out the sheet of notepaper and begins to speak, the music fading under the lines.*

HELENE (*the second syllable rhymes with* rain *or* Spain): Fourteen East Ninety-fifth Street, New York City, New York. October fifth, 1949, to Marks and Company, 84 Charing Cross Road, London W.C. Two, England! (*Lights coming up on Frank Doel*) Gentlemen! Your ad in the *Saturday Review of Literature* (*Frank slits open her letter with paper knife, looks at the address and reads*) says that you specialize in out-of-print books. The phrase "antiquarian booksellers" scares me somewhat, as I equate "antique" with "expensive." I am a poor writer with an antiquarian taste in books and all the things I want are impossible to get over here except in very expensive rare editions or in Barnes and Noble's grimy, marked-up schoolboy copies. (*Lights come up on rest of shop. Megan is at work at table up-stage center in alcove. Cecily is standing on the step-ladder consulting a book*) I enclose a list of my most pressing problems. If you (*Frank Doel is making notes of her requests*) have any clean secondhand copies of any of the books on the list, for no more than five dollars each, will you consider this a purchase order and send them to me. Very truly yours . . . (*Megan looks up, as though to register the name*) Helene Hanff. (*Pause*) *Miss* Helene Hanff!

FRANK: Dear Madam: In reply to your letter of October fifth we have managed to clear up two thirds of your problem. (*Megan is crossing to him with the Stevenson and the Hazlitt, then returns to her table. Cecily will then move downstage to center stage table to look for the Bibles—she has two in her hands but is searching for others*) The three Hazlitt essays you want are contained in the Nonesuch Press edition of his selected essays, and the Stevenson is found in *Virginibus Pueris-que*. We are sending nice copies of both these by book post . . . (*Having checked them he lets Megan take them upstage to make an invoice*) and we trust that they will arrive safely in due course and that you will be pleased with them. Our invoice is enclosed with the books. (*Megan rings bell and Bill enters. He stands at her side while she completes the invoice which she slips inside the top book and hands to him to take out to par-cel in the outer office*) The Leigh Hunt essays are not going to be so easy but we will see if we can find an at-tractive volume with them all in. (*Cecily is now stand-ing at his side with an armful of Bibles and he will se-lect the ones he wants. She then replaces the unwanted volumes*) We haven't the Latin Bible you describe but we have a Latin New Testament, also a Greek New Testament, ordinary modern editions in cloth binding.

Would you like these? (*Mr. Martin enters and takes Megan's place for whom she was standing in. She sits at table center stage, examining a volume. Cecily exits*)

HELENE: Gentlemen! The books arrived safely; the Robert Louis Stevenson is so fine it embarrasses my orange-crate bookshelves. I'm almost afraid to handle such soft vellum and heavy cream-colored pages. Being used to the dead-white paper and stiff cardboardy covers of American books, I never knew a book could be such a joy to touch. (*She puts down the Stevenson and crosses over to her sofa to get her handbag. She removes six dollars*) A Britisher whose girl lives upstairs translated the one pound seventeen six for me and says I owe you five dollars thirty for the two books. I hope he got it right. I enclose a five-dollar bill and a single . . . (*She has taken an airmail envelope and is putting the dollar bills inside*) . . . please use the seventy cents towards the price of the New Testaments, both of which I want. Will you please translate your prices hereafter? I don't add too well, in plain American I haven't a prayer of ever mastering bilingual arithmetic. (*During the laugh she licks gum of envelope flap*) Yours, Helene Hanff. (*She seals envelope and is about to drop it in her "box" when a thought strikes her . . .*) P.S. I hope "Madam" doesn't mean over there what it does here! (*Drops letter into "box"*)

FRANK: Dear *Miss* Hanff! We are very happy you liked the Stevenson so much . . . (*Megan looks up and moves across to Frank*) We are sending off the New Testaments, with an invoice listing the amount due in both pounds and dollars . . . (*He is handing the Bibles to Megan*) and we hope you will be pleased with them. (*Megan is moving away but on "six dollars," stops and turns back to take the dollars from Frank. They exchange a look of comic despair. Megan hands the dollars to Mr. Martin to enter up, he looks at them in curiosity as also does Cecily who returns at this moment.*)

Cecily takes the two books from Megan who has made out an invoice, standing at table beside Mr. Martin to do this. Megan then returns to table enter stage to carry on her work there) Your *six* dollars arrived safely . . . but we should feel very much easier if you would send your remittance by postal order in future as this would be quite a bit safer for you than entrusting dollar bills to the mails. Yours faithfully, F.P.D. (*Pause*) For Marks and Company.

HELENE (*Rising and moving to front of desk with the Bible*): What kind of a black Protestant Bible is this? Kindly inform the Church of England they have loused up the most beautiful prose ever written, whoever told them to tinker with the Vulgate Latin. They'll burn for it, you mark my words. It's nothing to me, I'm Jewish myself. But I have a Catholic sister-in-law, a Methodist sister-in-law, a whole raft of Presbyterian cousins (through my Great-Uncle—Abraham who converted) and an Aunt who's a Christian Science healer, and I like to think *none* of them would countenance this Anglican Latin Bible if they knew it existed. As it happens they don't know Latin existed. (*Mr. Martin exits*) Well, the hell with it. I've been using my Latin teacher's Vulgate, what I imagine I'll do is just not give it back till you find me one of my own. (*She takes dollars out of her wallet, takes an airmail envelope and puts dollars inside*) I enclose four dollars to cover the three dollars eighty-eight due to you, buy yourself a cup of coffee with the twelve cents. There's no post office near here and I'm not running all the way to Rockefeller Plaza to stand in line for a three-dollar-eighty-eight money order. If I wait till I get down there for something else, I won't have the three dollars eighty-eight anymore. I have implicit faith in the U.S. Airmail and His Majesty's Postal Service. (*She puts letter in "box," then checks her notebook at side of typewriter*) Have you got a copy of Landor's *Imaginary Conversations*?

(*Megan looks up at this*) I think there are several volumes; the one I want is the one with the Greek Conversations. (*There is a set of Landors on the table at which Megan is seated. She takes one, consults. Then takes another, checks the contents—it is the one with the Aesop and Rhodope conversations*) If it contains a dialogue between Aesop and Rhodope that'll be the volume I want. Yours, Helene Hanff. (*She seals envelope and drops it into the "box"*)

FRANK: Dear Miss Hanff: Your four dollars arrived safely and we have credited the twelve cents to your account. (*Megan rises, hands the volume to Frank. He checks it and takes it from Megan. She goes upstage*) We happen to have in stock Volume Two of the *Works and Life of Walter Savage Landor* which contains the Greek dialogues including the one mentioned in your letter, as well as the Roman dialogues. It is an old edition, published in 1876, not very handsome but well bound and a good clean copy, and we are sending it off today with invoice enclosed. (*He has moved upstage and handed the book to Megan who makes out invoice. He turns back*) I am sorry we made the mistake with the Latin Bible and will try to find a Vulgate for you. Not forgetting the Leigh Hunt. Yours faithfully, F.P.D. (*Pause*) For Marks and Company.

(*Megan slowly exits, taking the Landor with her*)

HELENE: December eighth, 1949. Sir: Well, it feels witless to keep writing "Gentlemen" when the same solitary soul is obviously taking care of everything for me. (*Frank reacts to this. Helene rises with the Landor and moves to sofa with it. Frank stands at side of desk, reading a catalog*) Savage Landor arrived safely and promptly fell open to a Roman dialogue where two cities had just been destroyed by a war and everybody was being crucified and begging passing Roman soldiers to run them through and end the agony. It'll be a relief to turn to Aesop and Rhodope where all you have to worry about is a famine. I do love secondhand books that open to the page some previous owner read oftenest. The day Hazlitt came he opened to "I hate to read new books" and I hollered "Comrade" to whoever owned it before me. I enclose a dollar . . . (*Frank looks up at this. Helene finds an envelope and puts it inside*) which Brian, British boy friend of Kay upstairs, says will cover the eight shillings I owe you, you forgot to translate! (*She moves front of desk. Frank quietly at work*) Now then! Brian told me you are all rationed to two ounces of meat per family per week and one egg per person per month and I am simply appalled. (*She ferrets among pile of scripts on floor and finds catalog. Kneels on floor*) He has a catalog from a British firm here which flies food from Denmark to his mother in England, so I am sending a small Christmas present to Marks and Company. I hope there will be enough to go round; he says the Charing Cross Road bookshops are all "quite small." I am sending it care of you, F.P.D., whoever you are. (*Music of "Jingle Bells." The others enter on the word "sending," led by Megan who holds a large cardboard box, covered with customs labels. They approach Frank, smiling and set box on table at side of his desk*) Noel, Helene Hanff. (*Music swells. Frank takes scissors and cuts string. They open the parcel—brightly colored Christmas-wrapped parcels emerge, then—on cue—Megan lifts out a large ham bound in muslin*) F.P.D.! CRISIS! I sent that package off. The chief item in it was a six-pound ham; I figured you could take it to a butcher and get it sliced up so everybody would have some to take home. But I just noticed on your invoice . . . (*Here the actors freeze, looking front, as though listening to Helene*) it says "B. Marks, M. Cohen, Proprietors." ARE THEY KOSHER? I could rush over a tongue. ADVISE PLEASE!

(*They all laugh*)

FRANK: Dear Miss Hanff: Just a note to let you know that
your gift parcel arrived safely and the contents have
been shared out between the staff. Mr. Marks and Mr.
Cohen insisted that we divide it up among ourselves
and not include the bosses. (*Music out. Frank at desk.
The others exiting. Cecily takes box from Megan who
sits at upstage table holding her share of the parcel.
Frank has a tin of jam, only the top of wrapping torn
off—so the tin is not identifiable. He moves to center
stage*) I should just like to add that everything in the
parcel was something that we either never see or can
only be had through the black market. It was extremely
kind of you to think of us in this way and we are all extremely grateful. We all wish to express our thanks and
send our greetings and best wishes for 1950. Yours
faithfully—Frank Doel. (*He turns to exit*)
HELENE: Frank Doel! (*F.D. swerves around quickly and
adds:*)
FRANK: For Marks and Company!

(*He exits, pausing en route to show Megan his present.
Helene continues working. She puts a piece of paper in
the machine and types. Light change—winter to spring.
She looks up*)

HELENE: Frank Doel? (*Pause. Sound of New York siren*)
Frank Doel? (*She pulls paper out of machine in despair, screws it up, and throws it on the floor. Rises*)
Frank Doel, what are you DOING over there, you are not
doing ANYTHING, you are just sitting AROUND. (*Frank
enters from outer office, holding H.H.'s latest letter. He
hurries to the desk for a paper knife and opens it. He
throws envelope in wastepaper basket. He reads the
letter with secretive delight*) Where is Leigh Hunt?

Where is the *Oxford Verse?* Where is the Vulgate and
dear goofy John Henry Newman. I thought they'd be
such nice uplifting reading for Lent and NOTHING do
you send me. You leave me sitting here writing long
margin notes in library books that don't belong to me;
someday they'll find out I did it and take my library
card away. (*She picks up the catalog*) I have made ar-
rangements with the Easter bunny to bring you an egg.
(*Frank looks up from reading the letter, entertained by
this*) He will get over there and find you have died of
INERTIA. (*She is removing her woolen jacket, and
drapes it around chair on next lines. She moves downstage of desk. She is at a low point*) I require a book of
love poems with spring coming on. No Keats or Shelley,
send me poets who can make love without slobbering—
Wyatt or Johnson or somebody, use your own judg-
ment. Just a nice book, preferably small enough to stick
in a slacks pocket and take to Central Park. (*Music for
"Easter Parade" heard on the phrase "as I came
through" the door. Frank is standing musing*) Well,
don't just sit there! Go find it! I swear I don't know how
that shop keeps going!

(*She starts to sing "In your Easter bonnet," as the music
swells, and types. Bill, Mr. Martin, and Cecily appear
with another parcel. Megan at her table, where she is
seated, snips the string with a pair of scissors. Frank is
watching. Megan joins the others in bringing the parcel
to him. They bring out Easter eggs, boxes of shell eggs—
wrapped—and an absurd duck, with a label round its
neck. Well, the duck looks real, but it's a jokey present
from H.H. to—yes, Megan reads the label and looks at
Frank. He points finger at his chest as though to say "For
me?" And Megan hands him the duck which he places on
desk. H.H. has stopped singing but the music swells.
Frank speaks over it, laughing*)

FRANK: Dear Miss Hanff: I have to thank you for the very welcome Easter parcel which arrived safely. We were all delighted to see the tins and the box of shell eggs, and the rest of the staff join me in thanking you . . . (*They all turn toward him, holding their gifts, and he conducts them like a chorus*)

ALL TOGETHER: for your very kind and generous thoughts of us! (*They exit*)

FRANK: I'm sorry we haven't been able to send you any of the books you want. (*Softly, from outside in the street, a barrel organ is heard playing. Frank is collecting his hat from the hatstand that stands left of the door, picks up his umbrella, and briefcase, and the box of shell eggs*) About the book of love poems, now and then we do get such a volume as you describe. We have none in stock at present but shall look out for one for you. Again, many thanks for the parcel. (*Cecily enters, stops abruptly when she sees Frank, and goes to stepladder, pretending to look for a book. Megan is no longer on stage*) Faithfully yours, Frank Doel. (*Pause*) For Marks and Company. (*He exits*)

(*Cecily slips over to window to check he has really gone, then comes down front. She is holding a clipboard and the letter she has written to H.H.*)

CECILY: Dear Miss Hanff! (*Helene looks up at this new voice*) Please don't let Frank know I'm writing this but every time I send you a bill I've been dying to slip in a little note and he might not think it quite proper of me. That sounds stuffy and he's not, he's quite nice really, very nice in fact, it's just that he does rather look on you as his private correspondent as all your letters and parcels are addressed to him. But I just thought I would write to you on my own. (*She sits on edge of table center stage*) We all love your letters and try to imagine what you must be like. I've decided you're young and very sophisticated and smart-looking. (*Helene makes a rueful moue at this remark*) Old Mr. Martin thinks you must be quite studious-looking in spite of your wonderful sense of humor. Why don't you send us a snapshot? (*Helene covers her face. Cecily crosses and stands behind Frank's desk*) If you're curious about Frank— (*Helene looks up at this, removing spectacles*) he's in his early forties, quite nice-looking; married to a very sweet Irish girl. I believe she's his second wife. (*She looks at toy duck and holds it in her arms*) Everyone was so grateful for the parcel. My little ones—girl five, boy four—were in Heaven. With the raisins and eggs I was able to make them a *cake!* I hope you don't mind my writing. (*She quietly puts back duck and returns to behind desk*) Please don't mention it when you write to Frank. With best wishes, Cecily Farr. (*She writes on back of envelope*) P.S. I shall put my home address on the back in case you should ever want anything sent to you from London.

HELENE (*Rising, hands in pockets, intrigued by this new development*): Dear Cecily— Tell Mr. Martin I'm so unstudious, I never went to college, I just happen to have peculiar tastes in books, thanks to a Cambridge professor named Quiller-Couch, known as Q, whom I fell over in a library when I was seventeen. And I'm about as smart-looking as a Broadway panhandler. (*She moves to behind desk, picks up woolen jacket, and moves front of desk again, putting it on, and rolling sleeves down over hands, shivering*) I live in moth-eaten sweaters and wool slacks; they don't give us any heat here in the daytime. It's a five-story brownstone and all the other tenants go out to work at nine a.m. and don't come home till six (*She shouts the following offstage*) and why should the landlord heat the building for one small script reader/writer working at home on the ground floor? (*Aside*) I bet he's got heat in his apartment! (*By now she is seated at her desk, ready for a morning's work. She leans forward, elbows on desk*) Poor Frank, I give him such a hard time, I'm always bawling him out for something. I'm only teasing, but I know he'll take me seriously. I keep trying to puncture that proper British reserve; if he gets ulcers I did it. Please write and tell me about London. I live for the day when I step off the boat train and feel its dirty sidewalks under my feet. I want to walk up Berkeley Square and down Wimpole Street and stand in St. Paul's where John Donne preached and sit on the step Elizabeth sat on when she refused to enter the Tower, and like that. A newspaperman I know, who was stationed in England during the war, says tourists go to England with preconceived notions, so they always find what they go looking for. I told him I'd go looking for the England of English literature, and he said, "Then it's all there."

(*Frank, carrying briefcase and umbrella enters at that moment and overhears Cecily reading end of her letter from H.H.:*)

CECILY: Regards, Helene Hanff.

(*Cecily, guiltily, crosses to table center stage, dropping several letters en route. She hurries off upstage, bumping into Mr. Martin who enters at that moment. Mr. Martin turns, looks after her, shaking his head. Mr. Martin sits at his work. Frank is carrying two books, one of which is wrapped in tissue paper. He looks at Cecily, and at Mr. M. and plays up to "Anyway" in indignation at Cecily's behavior*)

FRANK: Dear Miss Hanff: It is such a long time since we wrote to you I hope you do not think we have forgotten all about your wants. (*Puts down briefcase on table at side of desk*) Anyway, I have now managed to find for you the *Oxford Book of English Verse,* printed on India paper, original blue cloth binding, 1905, inscription in ink on the flyleaf, but a good secondhand copy, price two dollars. (*Megan is entering, reading a letter from a customer. She checks along the shelves*) We thought we had better quote before sending, in case you have already purchased a copy. (*He puts down the Oxford University Press book and handles now the book wrapped in tissue. He moves front of desk to center stage*) Some time ago you asked us for Newman's *Idea of a University.* Would you be interested in a copy of the first edition? Price six dollars. (*He holds out the book teasingly. H.H. stares front, mesmerized. The bait has taken!*) In case you would like them, we will put both books on one side until you have time to reply.

(*Helene rises, in a state of high excitement, snatching handbag from sofa, then searching for money hidden, squirrel-like, in tins on her desk, in a mug. She shovels the dollars into envelope*)

HELENE: He has a first edition of Newman's *University* for six bucks, do I want it? he asks innocently. Dear Frank, Yes, I want it! (*Frank looks up, grins, then exits with the books*) I won't be fit to live with myself. I've never cared about first editions per se, but a first edition of *that* book!—oh, my! I can just see it. (*Activity among the tins*) Send the *Oxford Verse* too. Never wonder if I've found something somewhere else any more. Why should I run all the way to Seventeenth Street, to buy dirty, badly made books when I can buy clean, beautiful ones from you without leaving the typewriter? From where I sit, London's a lot closer than Seventeenth Street.

(*Cecily is entering upstage, she hesitates, then sits at table downstage next to Frank's desk. She is pretending*) *to read a book. Megan, standing at shelves upstage, reading, observes her)*

HELENE (*Stuffs dollars into an envelope*): Enclosed please God please find eight dollars. Did I tell you about Brian? He buys physics tomes from a technical bookshop in London. He's not sloppy and haphazard like me. He bought an expensive set and went to Rockefeller Plaza and stood in line and got a money order and cabled it or whatever you do with it. He's a businessman, he does things right. The money order got lost in transit! *Up* His Majesty's Postal Service. (*She drops the letter into her "box"*)

(*Cecily looks up, and brings out from cover of book she is pretending to read, an envelope and some snapshots. Helene will have an identical set of these photos*)

CECILY: Dear Helene, I brought the enclosed snapshots to the shop with me weeks ago, but we've been frightfully busy so have had no chance to send them. They were taken in Norfolk where Doug (my husband) is stationed with the RAF. (*Megan, who is anxious for Cecily, overhears this*) None of them are very flattering of me, but they are the best we have of the children and the one of Doug alone is very good. (*Helene is looking at the snapshots. Megan, turning page of her book, crosses slowly to Frank's desk*) My dear, I do hope you get your wish to come to England. Why not save your pennies and come to England next summer? Mummy and Daddy have a house in Middlesex and would be delighted to put you up. (*Helene rises thoughtfully, moving front, considering this*) Megan Wells (*Cecily looks up at Megan and they smile*) and I are going on a week's holiday to Jersey in July. Megan is secretary to the bosses. Why don't you come with us and then you could economize the rest of the month in Middle-

sex. (*During the last sentence, Mr. Martin has risen
and with the ledger is about to ask Megan a question
but notices Cecily—gossiping as it were. Megan at once
distracts his attention, signaling "Beware!" to Cecily,
and guides Mr. Martin upstage, talking to him*) Mr.
Martin is trying to see what I'm writing so shall have to
close. Sincerely, Cecily.

(*Frank Doel is entering in a hurry with H.H.'s latest letter but his way is blocked by Megan and Mr. Martin.
They part. At the same time, her head down, Cecily is
hurrying out and collides with them. She exits. Mr. Martin again shakes his head at her. He'll have to speak to her
and he follows her out. Megan returns with her book to
bookcase where she stands reading it. Frank sits
with latest letter at table where Cecily has been sitting.
Helene has risen with a leather-bound book in one hand
and two large pages from Clarendon Press, with creases
in them*)

HELENE: WELL!! All I have to say to YOU, Frank Doel, is
we live in depraved, destructive and degenerate times
when a bookshop—a BOOKSHOP—starts tearing up beautiful old books to use as wrapping paper. I said to Car-
dinal Newman when he stepped out of it: Would you
believe a thing like that, John Henry . . . And he said
he wouldn't. You tore that book up in the middle of a
major battle and I don't even know WHICH WAR IT WAS!
(*Frank looks up in delight. Helene puts down wrapping on desk and moves to sofa with the Newman*) The
Newman arrived almost a week ago and I'm just beginning to recover. I keep it on the table with me all day;
every now and then I stop typing and reach over and
touch it. Not because it's a first edition; I just never saw
a book so beautiful . . .
   I feel vaguely guilty about owning it. (*Frank has
been glowing all through this. Suddenly he senses*

Megan watching him. He turns to look back at her with a shy smile. Then she goes on reading and H.H. picks up Newman and puts it on her shelves) All that gleaming leather and gold stamping and beautiful type belongs in the pine-paneled library of an English country home; it wants to be read by the fire in a gentleman's leather easy chair—not on a secondhand studio couch in a one-room hovel in a broken-down brownstone front. (*Megan moves to table upstage center and sits. She has found the reference she was looking for. Helene rises, goes back to desk*) I want the Q anthology. (*She picks up the wrapping*) Why don't you wrap it in pages LCXII and LCXIII so I can at least find out who won the battle and what war it was? (*Frank laughs silently*) P.S. Have you got Sam Pepys' (*pronounced by H.H. "Peppis"*) Diary over there? I need him for long winter evenings.

(*Frank puts glasses in pocket and letter in inside pocket. Megan rings bell. Bill enters*)

FRANK: Dear Miss Hanff: I am sorry for the delay in answering your letter but I have been out of town for a week or so and am now busy trying to catch up on my correspondence. (*Megan is at table making out invoice for Bill. Frank is putting her last letter inside his coat pocket and rising*) Please don't worry about us using old books such as Clarendon's *Rebellion* for wrapping. In this particular case they were just two odd volumes with the covers detached and nobody in their right senses would have given us a shilling for them. (*Helene looks up in amazement at this. Obviously thinks they are out of their minds. She shrugs and goes on writing*) About the Sir Roger de Coverley Papers . . . (*Bill exits. Frank is moving toward a pile of books on the floor and here he will find the de Coverley*) . . . we happen to have in stock a volume of eighteenth-

century essays which includes a good selection of them
as well as essays by Chesterfield and Goldsmith. It is
edited by Austin Dobson (*He checks this and hands to
Megan, who reaches out to take it—but he withdraws
it to look at it again*) and is quite a nice edition and
as it is only one dollar fifteen we are sending it off to
you by book post. (*He hands it finally to Megan and
crosses to round table stage left*) The Quiller-Couch
anthology, *The Pilgrim's Way,* is being sent to you in
the same parcel. The balance due is— (*He hesitates*)
—one dollar eighty-five (*He hands this second book to
Megan and rings bell*) so your two dollars more than
covered it. We haven't a copy of Pepys' Diary in stock
at the moment but shall look out for one for you. (*He
is at the door*) There are six of us in the shop, not including Mr. Marks and Mr. Cohen. With best wishes,
F. Doel. For Marks and Company. (*He exits*)

CECILY: Helene, my dear— (*Cecily coming down ladder
and moving to crate*) There are many ways of doing it
but Mummy and I think this is the simplest for you to
try. (*H.H. gets up and puts on apron, while listening to the recipe*) Put a cup of flour, an egg, half a cup
of milk, and a good shake of salt into a large bowl and
beat all together until it is the consistency of thick
cream. Put in the fridge for several hours. It's best if
you make it in the morning. When you put your roast
in the oven, put in an extra pan to heat. Half an hour
before your roast is done, pour a bit of the roast grease
into the baking pan, just enough to cover the bottom
will do. The pan must be *very hot.* Now pour the pudding in and the roast and pudding will be ready at the
same time. (*H.H. goes to exit to kitchen, but is arrested
by next line*) I don't quite know how to describe it to
someone who has never seen it, but a good Yorkshire
pudding will puff up very high and brown and crisp
and when you cut into it you will find that it is . . . hol-
low inside. (*H.H. exits on the laugh and Cecily breaks*

to behind desk) The RAF is still keeping Doug in Norfolk and we are firmly hoarding your Christmas tins until he comes home, but oh, my dear, what a celebration we shall have when he does! I do think you oughtn't to spend your money like that. (*Cecily snatches up letter*) Must fly and post this if you're going to have it for Brian's birthday dinner, do let me know if it's a success. Love, Cecily.

(*Helene reenters, without apron, carrying mug of coffee*)

HELENE: Dear Cecily, Yorkshire pudding out of this world! (*Cecily goes to Megan to share this latest letter with her*) We have nothing like it. I had to describe it to somebody as a high, curved, smooth, empty waffle. (*She picks up the food catalog and sits on sofa. Cecily slowly drifts to down center table and sits reading the letter. When it gets to description of parcels, Megan will join her, standing looking over her shoulder, also reading the letter*) Please don't worry about what the food parcels cost; I don't know whether Overseas Association is nonprofit or duty free or what, but they are monstrous cheap; that whole Christmas parcel cost less than my turkey. They do have a few rich parcels with things like standing rib roasts and legs of lamb, but even those are so cheap compared with what they cost in the butcher shops that it kills me not to be able to send them. I have such a time with the catalog, I spread it out on the rug and debate the relative merits of Parcel 105 (includes one dozen eggs and a tin of sweet biscuits) and Parcel 217B (two dozen eggs and no sweet biscuits)—I hate the one-dozen-egg parcels. What is two eggs for anybody to take home? And no sweet biscuits? So it's a problem. (*Bill enters and puts mail down on upstage table. Megan and Cecily invite Bill to share in H.H.'s latest letter. He joins them*) A producer who likes my plays, but not enough to produce them, just phoned. He's producing a TV series, do I want to write for television? "Two bills," he said carelessly, which it turned out means two hundred dollars. And me a forty-dollar-a-week script-reader! I go down to see him tomorrow, keep your fingers crossed . . . Best, Helene. (*She types*)

(*The three cross their fingers. Megan crosses to Frank's desk; Cecily to chair at table at side of desk; while behind books Bill sits writing his letter at the center stage table. Each is writing unknown to the other*)

CECILY (*Writing letter*): Helene dear, your marvelous Easter parcels arrived safely and everyone is quite upset because Frank left the city on business for the firm the next morning and so hasn't written to thank you, and of course no one else quite dares to write to Frank's Miss Hanff. Love, Cecily. (*She exits quickly*)

(*Helene puts down her letter and almost at once is picking up Megan's letter. Megan is writing swiftly as she speaks, voice low, looking round quickly to check no one is watching*)

MEGAN: Dear Miss Hanff: This is just to let you know that your Easter parcels to Marks and Company arrived safely a few days ago but have not been acknowledged as Frank Doel is away from the office on business for the firm. (*She looks round her, then continues in an even quieter voice. She moves away from desk, slightly center, very confidential*) I did feel I must write and tell you how exceedingly grateful we all are for your kindness and generosity. We all hope that you will be able to come to England one of these days. We should do our best to make your trip a happy one. (*She looks round*) Sincerely, Megan Wells. (*She hurries out with her letter*)

(*Immediately, as Bill speaks, Helene picks up the third letter. Bill takes a quick look round first, before speaking*)

BILL (*Rising*): Dear Miss Hanff: For nearly two years I have been working as a cataloger at Marks and Company and would like to thank you very much for my share-out in the parcels which you've been sending. (*He moves to Frank's desk, picking up mail*) I live with my great aunt who is seventy-five, and I think that if you had seen the look of delight on her face when I brought home the meat and the tin of tongue, you would have realized just how grateful we are. (*He moves downstage to pick up two books on the crate*) It's certainly good to know that someone so many miles away can be so kind and generous to people they haven't even seen . . . (*He begins to exit*) . . . and I think that everyone in the firm feels the same. Sincerely, Bill Humphries. (*He exits swiftly and simultaneously*)

(*Frank Doel enters swiftly from the street with hat, briefcase, and umbrella. With hand on door he speaks at once —so as to time the big laugh coming*)

FRANK: Dear Miss Hanff: I expect you are getting a bit worried that we have not written to thank you for your parcels—thinking that we are an ungrateful lot. (*Laugh*) (*Helene raises the four letters with amusement*) The truth is that I have been chasing round the country . . . (*He is closing door, hanging up hat and umbrella, and placing case on table*) . . . in and out of various stately homes of England trying to buy a few books to fill up our sadly depleted stocks. My wife was starting to call me the lodger who just went home for bed and breakfast, but of course when I arrived home with a nice piece of M-E-A-T, to say nothing of dried eggs and ham, then she thought I was a fine fellow and

all was forgiven. I must say it is a long time since we
saw so much meat all in one piece. (*He is now downstage center*) We should like to express our appreci-
ation in some way or other, so we are sending you by
book post today . . . (*He is removing from his jacket
pocket a small book. Simultaneously, H.H. is picking up
an identical book*) a little book which I hope you will
like. (*Simultaneously they are moving toward each
other, each holding a book. Facing front, they are now
very close*) I remember you asked me for a volume of
Elizabethan love poems some time ago—well, this is the
nearest I can get to it.

(*Helene removes from it a small card which she reads*)

HELENE: To Helene Hanff . . .
FRANK: With best wishes and grateful thanks for many
kindnesses from . . . (*He pauses, he would like to send
it from himself but . . .*) all at 84 Charing Cross Road,
London, April 1951.
HELENE: Thank you for the beautiful book. I've never
owned a book before with pages edged all round in
gold. Would you believe it arrived on my birthday?
(*He looks up at this, moved. There are tears in her
eyes, but she holds them back. They are quite close, she
behind and above him, each turning the pages of a
small book. She looks again at the card*) I wish you
hadn't been so overcourteous about putting the inscription on a card instead of on the flyleaf. It's the book-
seller coming out in you all, you were afraid you'd
decrease its value. You would have increased it for the
present owner. And possibly for the future owner. I
love inscriptions on fly-leaves and notes in margins; I
like the comradely sense of turning pages someone else
turned, and reading passages someone long ago has
called my attention to. And why didn't you sign your
names? (*Frank slips the book in his pocket and turns to*

exit. He is halfway out when he is arrested by the next words and turns round) I expect Frank wouldn't let you, he probably doesn't want me writing love letters to anybody but him. (*Frank, caught out, shyly runs his finger round the inside of his collar and grins coyly. Swift exit. Helene is alone. Light change, as though a storm, the sky darkening. H.H. moves to the desk and lights a cigarette*) I send you greetings from America— faithless friend that she is, pouring millions into re-building Japan and Germany while letting England starve. Some day, God willing, I'll get over there and apologize personally for my country's sins (and by the time I come home my country will certainly have to apologize for mine). Thank you again for the beautiful book, I shall try very hard not to get gin and ashes all over it; it's really too fine for the likes of me! (*She moves upstage and slowly puts on her jacket. Music is now heard, the opening bars of* Fantasia on a theme by Thomas Tallis)

(*We see Maxine, elegantly dressed—large picture-frame hat—coming down the street. She pauses briefly to browse outside. Opens door, pauses as she takes in the shop, moves center and music out as she speaks. We cannot see her face at first; the shop is full of shadows. The lights will come up slowly in her speech, on both sides of the stage. As she speaks, Helene turns front, and as speech starts will light a cigarette and lean against desk down-stage side, listening intently*)

MAXINE (*Played by the actress who plays Megan*): Dear-heart—it is the loveliest old shop straight out of Dickens, you would go absolutely out of your mind about it. There are stalls outside and I stopped and leafed through a few things just to establish myself as a browser before wandering in. It's dim inside, you smell the shop before you see it; it's a lovely smell, I can't articulate it easily but it combines must and dust and age, and walls of wood, and floors of wood. (*She moves upstage toward Mr. Martin's table*) Towards the back of the shop at the left there's a desk with a worklamp on it. A man was sitting there. He was about sixty, with a Hogarth nose. He looked up and said, "Good afternoon," in a North Country accent, and I said I just wanted to browse and he said please do. The shelves go on forever. They go up to the ceiling— (*She is now moving downstage center*) and they're very old and kind of gray, like old oak that has absorbed so much dust over the years they no longer are their true color. There's a print section with Cruikshank and Rackham and Spy and all those old wonderful English caricaturists and illustrators that I'm not smart enough to know a lot about, and there are some lovely old, old illustrated magazines. (*She sits on a hamper downstage center with one of the magazines*) I stayed for about half an hour hoping your Frank or one of the girls would turn up, but it was one-ish when I went in. I gather they were all out to lunch and I couldn't stay any longer. (*She makes up her mind to buy one for Helene*) As you will see, the notices for our play were not sensational, but we're told they're good enough to assure us a few months' run, so—yesterday—I went apartment hunting and found a nice little "bed-sitter" in Knightsbridge! I don't have the address here, I'll send it or—you can call my mother. (*She rises, looks for somewhere to put coins, crosses to Frank's desk and rests her handbag on it. She puts coins in the duck's back—which we now realize is a money box*) We have no food problems, we eat in restaurants and hotels; the best places like Claridge's get all the roast beef and chops they want. The prices are astronomical but the exchange rate is so good we can afford it. Of course, if I were English I would loathe us, instead of which they are absolutely wonderful to us; we're invited to everybody's home and everybody's club. The only thing we can't get is sugar or sweets in any form, for which I personally thank God. I intend to lose pounds over here. (*Helene laughs*) Write me, Love—Maxine.

HELENE: Maxine, bless your golden heart, what a peachy description, you write better than I do. (*She moves behind desk prior to putting out cigarette*) I don't like to sound bitter but I would like to know what YOU ever did that the good Lord lets YOU browse around my bookshop while I'm stuck on Ninety-fifth Street, writing the TV Adventures of Ellery Queen. (*Maxine laughs. Helene stubs out cigarette*) Did I tell you we're not allowed to use a lipstick-stained cigarette for a clue? (*She holds up her stub. She picks up an ashtray and will come round stage left of desk to empty it in bin under desk at front*) We're sponsored by the Bayuk Cigar Company and we're not allowed to mention the word cigarette. We can have ashtrays on the set but they can't have any cigarette butts in them. They can't have cigar butts either, they're not pretty. (*She returns empty ashtray to desk*) All an ashtray can have in it is a wrapped, unsmoked Bayuk cigar. (*The music of Eric Coates' London Suite—Knightsbridge—is heard. Helene moves front, hands in pockets*) And you hobnobbing with Gielgud at Clairidge's. Write me about London, the tube, the Inns of Court, Mayfair, the corner where the Globe Theatre stood, anything, I'm not fussy. (*Maxine moves to door of shop and turns on the word Knightsbridge*) Write me about Knightsbridge, it sounds green and gracious in Eric Coates' *London Suite.*

(*Maxine blows a kiss. She slowly exits, taking a last lingering look at the interior of shop. Closes door. Goes down street. Music still playing. Helene returns to her work, finds the Pepys' Diary that has just arrived and flicks through it, suddenly shutting the book with a bang —and the music stops abruptly*)

HELENE: Mr. Doel! WHAT KIND OF A PEPYS' DIARY DO YOU CALL THIS? This is not Pepys' Diary, this is some busy-body editor's miserable collection of EXCERPTS from Pepys' Diary may he rot. I could just spit. (*Frank Doel enters in a hurry, agitated, holding her letter which, underneath, has two dollars clipped to it. He grabs his spectacles from desk and comes down front, reading*) Where is January twelfth, 1688, where his wife chased him out of bed and around the bedroom with a red-hot poker?

FRANK: Miss Farr!!!!

(*Cecily hurries on, Frank glares at her, she looks guilty. She stands by him*)

HELENE: Where is Sir William Penn's son that was giving everybody so much trouble with his Quaker notions? ONE mention does he get in this whole pseudo book. And me from Philadelphia! (*She moves upstage*) I en-close two limp singles. (*Frank looks, finds them, de-taches them and hands them at arm's length to Cecily as though she were responsible*) I will make do with this thing until you find me a real Pepys'. THEN I will tear up this ersatz book, page by page, and WRAP THINGS IN IT! (*Frank sinks onto crate center stage*) Fresh eggs or powdered for Christmas? (*Frank, sur-prised by her sudden change of tone, looks round at Cecily who is upstage by worktable. She looks at him, laughs and exits*) I know the powdered last longer but "fresh eggs flown from Denmark" have to taste better. You want to take a vote on it?

(*Frank speaking very swiftly, to make amends. He is in a manic state of guilt and quite distraught. Very fast . . . Helene listens intently, to see what excuses he comes out with*)

FRANK: Dear Miss Hanff, First of all let me apologize for the Samuel Pepys' Diary. I was honestly under the impression that it was the complete Braybrooke edition and I can understand how you must have felt when you found your favorite passages missing. I promise to look at the next reasonably priced copy that comes along and if it contains the passages you mention in your letter I will send it along. (*Bill enters with two crates of books on a trolley, followed by Cecily with an armful of books and Megan with a checklist. They are all in a panic. They have never seen Frank like this before*) I am glad to say, I am very glad to say, I have managed to dig out a few books for you from a private library that we have just bought. (*Megan and Cecily are now downstage right, sorting books on a low table. Bill still unloading. As Frank approaches, Cecily hands him the Leigh Hunt*) There is a Leigh Hunt (*He holds it up in triumph*) which includes most of the essays you like. (*He is now standing between the two girls*) There is also a Vulgate New Testament (*He holds it up in triumph*) which I hope will be okay. (*He assumes an American accent for this. The two girls are amazed. Pause. He charges across stage left in search of more books*) I have also included a Dictionary to the Vulgate . . . (*He cannot find it, so Megan darts offstage left to see if she can find it in a smaller crate there. Frank now center stage. Bill joins Cecily with more books for sorting*) . . . which you might find useful. There is also a volume of twentieth-century English essays, though it contains only one by Hilaire Belloc—and nothing to do with bathrooms. (*Megan does a double-take at this non sequitur, then breaks upstage to the table center stage. Frank moves off left in front of desk*) Enclosed is our invoice for seventeen shillings and sixpence or approximately . . . (*In his excitement and guilt he still can't think clearly*)

(*Megan looks up, eyebrows raised, and prompts him*)

MEGAN: Two dollars fifty!

FRANK (*Still bemused*): Two dollars fifty! All that is due
to us on the books, as you had a credit balance with us
of nearly two dollars. (*Frank is now behind his desk,
holding the books. He looks across at the others, almost
absentmindedly; as he speaks about them, they look
up*) About the eggs—I have talked to the rest of the *inmates* here, and we all seem to think that the fresh ones
would be nicer . . . as you say, they will not last
as long, but they will taste . . . ah . . . much, ah
much . . .

MEGAN: Better!

(*They nod in agreement*)

FRANK: Yes . . . better . . . We are all hoping for better
things after the General Election. If Churchill and
Company get in, as I think and hope they will, it will
cheer everyone up immensely. (*He begins to exit upstage*) With best wishes, Yours sincerely, Frank Doel.
(*He is hurrying off but the others arrest him*)

OTHERS (*Aghast*): For Marks and Company!

(*Frank stops and adds:*)

FRANK: For Marks and Company! (*Exit*)

(*The others follow Frank out, Bill last with the trolley.
Helene seated at desk, holding two books, identical to
those we have just seen*)

HELENE: Dear Speed! You dizzy me, rushing Leigh Hunt
and the Vulgate over here whizbang like that. You
probably don't realize it but it's hardly more than two
years since I ordered them. You keep going at this rate

you're gonna give yourself a heart attack. (*Light change to winter*) That's mean. You just go to so much trouble for me and I never even thank you. I just needle you, it's mean. I really am grateful for all the pains you take for me. (*She has put the two books down on sofa and now goes back to desk to find the money and an envelope. The mug of coffee is standing on top of the dollars*) I enclose three dollars. Sorry about the top one. I spilled coffee on it and it wouldn't sponge off, but I think it's still good. You can still read it. (*We hear the beginning of "Unto Us a Child Is Born" from Handel's* Messiah) Do you carry hardcover vocal scores, by any chance? Like Bach's *St. Matthew's Passion* and Handel's *Messiah*? I could probably get them here at Schirmer's, but they're fifty cold blocks from where I live so I thought I'd ask you first. (*The envelope is now sealed and she drops it into her "box." She comes round to side of desk and, stooping down, picks up a bottle of gin from the floor and a glass. She puts glass on desk, unscrews bottle*) Congratulations on Churchill and Company, I hope he loosens up your rations a little. (*Pours drink. She lifts glass*) Is your name Welsh? (*She exits*)

(*Music swells. From upstage center a loud burst of squeakers. Frank enters unsteadily, wearing a paper hat, carrying glass of wine. He goes to chair*)

FRANK: December fifteenth, 1951. Dear Miss Hanff! You will be glad to know that two boxes of eggs and the tins of tongue have all arrived safely and once again we all wish to thank you most sincerely for your extreme generosity. (*There is a loud burst of squeakers. Enter Megan, Bill, and Cecily in party paper hats. Bill also wears a false nose and carries a sprig of mistletoe. They push Cecily, who kisses Frank on the cheek. They laugh and blow squeakers again. It is the middle of the office party! He realizes he has got lipstick on his cheek. He puts down glass on table at side of his desk, and gets out a handkerchief to wipe off lipstick. The others, watching from upstage, blow squeakers again, he turns, waving them off, and they go out)* Mr. Martin, one of the older members of our staff, has been on the sick list for some time and we therefore let him have— *(Here, in picking up his glass, he accidentally knocks two small books onto the floor. He looks round guiltily)* Oh, dear!— *(and picks them up)* the lion's share of the eggs, one whole boxful in fact, and of course he was delighted to get them. The tins of tongue look very inviting and will be a welcome addition to our larders, and in my case will be put on one side for a special occasion. *(The three enter with a large cardboard box and Megan has sticky labels to stick on it)* We are sending you a little gift for Christmas. *(Music out)* It is linen and we hope that you will not have to pay duty on it. We will mark it . . . *(He pauses, at a loss. Megan prompts him)*

MEGAN: Christmas gift!

FRANK: . . . Christmas gift—and keep our fingers crossed. *(Bill exits to post parcel)* Anyway, we hope you will like it and accept it with our sincere best wishes for Christmas . . . *(He pauses. Megan and Cecily chorus: ". . . and the coming year")* . . . and the coming year. *(Frank lurches to behind his desk and, leaning over it, still holding his glass, says belligerently)* My name is certainly not of Welsh origin. As it is pronounced to rhyme with the French word "Noel"— *(Megan and Cecily start to sing "The First Noel," quietly sending him up. Frank looks up amused)* I think there may be a possibility that it originated in France!

(He joins in the singing, conducting them. At the end of the fourth line they hum and over this Helene reenters

with Christmas card in one hand, box, minus cover, in other)

HELENE: Christmas greetings and all good wishes for the New Year from George Martin . . .
CECILY: Cecily Farr.
MEGAN: Megan Wells.
FRANK: Frank Doel!

(Bill slithers back just in time)

BILL: William Humphries!
HELENE: J. Pemberton?

(In the shop they sing a chorus of four noels. Frank collects the paper hats, and exits with Bill. Megan sits upstage center, and Cecily sits upstage end of center table. H.H. removes tablecloth from box)

HELENE: Maxine! Wait till you see what the shop sent me for Christmas! It's an Irish linen tablecloth, the color of thick cream, hand-embroidered in an old-fashioned pattern of leaves and flowers, every flower worked in a different color and shaded from very pale to very deep. You never saw anything like it. My junk-shop drop-leaf table *certainly* never saw anything like it. I get this urge . . . *(She is pouring out gin, and pours it like tea from a teapot)* to shake out my flowing Victorian sleeve and lift a graceful arm to pour tea from an imaginary Georgian teapot; we're gonna play Stanislavski with it the minute you get home. *(She exits with cloth and box and glass)*

(Frank enters from back of shop, crosses to desk)

FRANK: Seventeenth January 1952. Dear Miss Hanff, First of all we're so glad that you liked the cloth. It gave us a

lot of pleasure to send it and it was one little way of
thanking you for all your kind gifts over the last few
years. You may be interested to know that it was em-
broidered, quite recently, by an old lady of over eighty
who lives in the flat—ah! *apartment!* next door to me.
She lives all by herself and does quite a lot of needle-
work as a hobby. She does not often part with any of
her work, but my wife managed to persuade her to sell
this cloth, and I think she also made her a present of
some of the dried egg you sent us which helped a lot.
(*He has collected hat, briefcase and umbrella*) If you
must wash your Bible . . . we should advise ordinary
soap and water. Put a teaspoon of soda in a pint of
warm water . . . and use a soapy sponge. I think you
will find this will remove the dirt . . . and you can then
polish it with a little lanolin! (*He exits by shop door*)

(*H.H. lifts two or three scripts and waves them*)

HELENE: Maxine! The Ellery Queen series raised me to
two hundred and fifty dollars a script. If it keeps up till
June, I may get to England and browse around my
bookshop myself. If I have the nerve. I write them the
most outrageous letters from a safe three thousand
miles away. I'll probably walk in there one day and
walk right out again without telling them who I am.
(*She moves downstage*) I fail to see why you did not
understand that grocery man in Knightsbridge. He did
not call it "ground ground nuts." He called it "ground
ground-nuts" which is the only *sensible* thing to call it.
Peanuts grow in the *ground* and are therefore *ground-*
nuts, and after you have taken them out of the ground
you grind them up and you have *ground* ground-nuts,
which is a much more accurate name than peanut but-
ter. You just don't understand English. Kisses, H.
Hanff, girl etymologist! (*She turns, then swings back*)
P.S. I have just talked to your mother. She says you

don't think the show in London will run another month and she says you took two dozen pairs of nylons over there, so do me a favor. As soon as the closing notice goes up, take four pairs of nylons around to the bookshop for me, give them to Frank Doel, tell him they're for the three girls and Nora, his wife.

(*On the words "closing notice" Cecily checks watch, rises, goes to door, turns* OPEN *sign round to* CLOSED, *locks door. Over to Megan—it's time to go to funeral—and both exit*)

HELENE: Frank Doel, thou *sloth!* I could *rot* over here before you'd send me anything to read. You may add Walton's Lives to the list of books you aren't sending me. You can't even get Walton's Lives in a library over here. You can look at it. They have it down at the Forty-second branch. But not to take *home!* The lady said to me, shocked. *Read it here.* Just sit down in room 315 and read the whole book without a cup of coffee, a cigarette, or air.

(*Sound of church bells. From the street a procession appears. Frank opens door, and William appears first, with a black mourning band on his arm. Megan follows with a black hat, and Cecily with a black scarf over her head. Cecily reverses sign. Frank carries, as usual, his hat, briefcase, and umbrella. He has a black mourning band also on his arm. Bill exits. The girls, slowly removing headgear, look at Frank, then Cecily exits to make coffee for them*)

HELENE: What do you do with yourself all day? Sit in the back of the store and read? Why don't you try selling a book to somebody? *Miss* Hanff to you—I'm Helene only to my *friends*. (*She sits behind desk, putting on her glasses*) P.S. Tell the girls and Nora if all goes well they're getting nylons for Lent.

(*Frank is now behind his desk*)

FRANK: Dear Helene! (*Helene looks up at this. At last! Then continues with her work*) I quite agree it is time we dropped the "Miss" when writing to you. I am not really so standoffish, as you may have been led to believe, but as copies of the letters I have written to you go into the office files the formal address seemed more appropriate. But as this letter has nothing to do with books, there will be no copy. We are quite at a loss to know how you managed the nylons, which appeared this noon as if by magic. All I can tell you is that when I came back from lunch they were on my desk with a note reading, "From Helene Hanff." (*Enter Cecily with the coffee on tray, three cups, and puts down tray on table. Takes her own cup and saucer. Megan carries the sugar bowl and a spoon*) No one seems to know how or when they arrived. (*He looks across at the girls*) The girls are very thrilled and I believe they are planning to write to you themselves. (*Megan hands him his cup and puts a spoonful of sugar in it for him. Pause. Cecily goes to sit at head of center stage table with her coffee*) I am sorry to say that our friend Mr. George Martin, who has been so ill for some time, passed away in hospital last week. He was with the firm a great number of years, so what with his loss and the King dying so suddenly as well, we are rather a mournful crowd at present. (*He moves away with his cup, coming down front of desk. Megan gives Cecily a look, and stands sipping her coffee*) I don't see how we can ever repay you for your many kind gifts. All I can say is, if ever you decide to make the trip to England, there will be a bed for you at Thirty-seven Oakfield Court for as long as you care to stay. With all good wishes, *Frank!*

HELENE: Oh, my. (*Pause*) I do bless you for this Walton's Lives. It's incredible that a book published in 1840 can be in such perfect condition more than a hundred years later. Such beautiful, mellow, rough-cut pages they are. (*Cecily quietly exits and Megan sits at worktable sipping coffee. Frank still stands downstage holding his cup and saucer. H.H. moves downstage*) I do feel for poor William T. Gordon who wrote his name in it in 1841. What a crummy lot of descendants he must have—to sell it to you casually for nothing. Boy, I'd like to have run barefoot through *their* library before they sold it. Fascinating book to read. Did you know John Donne eloped with the boss's highborn daughter and landed in the Tower for it and starved and starved and *then* got religion, my word. (*H.H. puts book down on desk. Frank turns, puts cup down on desk, sees Megan watching, smiles. She resumes work. He to hatstand and quietly removes armband. Helene rising, crossing to sofa for handbag and taking out money*) Now listen, I'm enclosing a five-dollar bill. That Walton's Lives makes me very dissatisfied with my *Angler*, which I bought before I met you. So use the extra two-dollars-fifty for a nice English *Angler*, please. (*She drops letter into the "box" and settles back at work*) You better watch out. (*Frank is now back at his desk*) I'm coming over in fifty-three if Ellery is renewed. (*Frank looks up and across at Megan. They are excited*) I'm gonna climb up that Victorian book-ladder and disturb the dust on the top shelves and everybody's decorum. Or didn't I ever tell you I write arty murders for Ellery Queen on television? All my scripts have artistic backgrounds: ballet, concert hall, opera; and all the suspects *and* the corpses are cultured. Maybe I'll do one about the rare-book business in your honor—you want to be the murderer or the corpse?

(Frank lifts his file with a flourish. Opens desk and deposits file inside)

FRANK: Seventeenth April 1952, Dear Helene, You see I don't care about the files anymore! *(William enters with another trolley full of books followed by Megan and Cecily with armfuls of books. Cecily goes downstage right, Megan to center table, and Bill unpacks books at table to side of Frank's desk)* You will be pleased to know we have just purchased a private library which includes a very nice copy of Walton's *Compleat Angler*, and will be sending it to you today. *(He is putting away his files inside desk, and then picking up briefcase, and hat—a Panama this time—and umbrella from hatstand)* Your Ellery Queen scripts sound rather fun. I wish we could have the chance of seeing some of them on our TV over here—it wants livening up a bit. Our TV, I mean, not your script! *(He moves, holding Panama hat, to center stage)*

(Bill has just discovered an unusual first edition and draws Frank's attention to it. He will move on from Bill to Megan and down to Cecily, arriving by end of H.H. speech)

HELENE: Dear Frank, the woodcuts in Walton's *Angler* alone are worth ten times the price of the book. What a peculiar world we live in when so beautiful a thing can be owned for life or for the price of a ticket to a Broadway movie palace, or one fiftieth of having one tooth capped. Well, if your books cost what they're worth, I couldn't afford them. Regards to Nora and the wage slaves.

FRANK: August twenty-sixth 1952—Dear Helene, thirty volumes of Loeb Classics have come in, but, alas, no Horace, no Sappho, no Catullus. I am taking a couple of weeks' holiday— *(He puts on his Panama hat at a*

*jaunty angle walking across front of stage; the others
listen*) but as I have just bought a car we are com-
pletely broke so we'll have to take things easy. Nora has
a sister who lives by the sea so we are hoping she will
take pity on us and invite us to stay with her. It is my
first car, so we are all very thrilled with it—even though
it is an old 1939 model. So long as it gets us to places
without breaking down too often we shall be quite
happy. With all good wishes, Frank Doel! (*Umbrella at
an angle, like a rifle, he strides off. The others resume
work. Helene looks up*)

HELENE: Hey, Frankie! How about if I came over next
year in time for the Coronation? (*She starts typing*)

(*We hear the honk and starting noises of the car. As a
joke, Bill starts to sing "My Old Man Says Follow the
Van!" Megan and Cecily pick this up, and cross to shop
window, their arms full of books, and watch Frank drive
off. Megan and Cecily exit upstage center on "Old Cock
Linnit." H.H. starts singing "Over there . . . the Yanks
are coming!" Bill is waving*)

END OF ACT ONE

ACT TWO

ACT TWO

Inside the shop, Frank in a linen jacket is showing the others snapshots of his holiday. They are in a group center stage. The wooden crate has been moved from center stage to stage left.

The curtain rises to the music of "On the Town" outside the shop windows; bunting is hung, ready for the Coronation. Bill now wears a tweed jacket.

Helene enters at a climax in the music, carrying a cardboard box—she is spring-cleaning her books.

HELENE: Hey, Frankie! Guess who came while you were away on vacation? Sam Pepys! (*Music out. She pauses to touch the three slim volumes on her desk. Those in shop disperse to sorting and rearranging books*) Please thank whoever mailed him; he came a week ago. He stepped out of three pages of some tabloid, three honest navy blue volumes of him. I read the tabloid over lunch and started Sam after dinner. (*Helene is stuffing books into the box. She checks titles, and occasionally decides not to throw one out*) He says to tell you he's overjoyed to be here; he was previously owned by a slob who never even bothered to cut the pages. I'm wrecking them; it's the thinnest onionskin paper I ever saw. But heavier paper would have taken up six or seven volumes and very few books left to throw out. (*Bill by now is working at table upstage. Cecily exits and Megan. Frank finishes arranging display on table center stage and exits in next line*) I house-clean my books every spring and throw out those I'm never going to read again like I throw out clothes I'm never going to wear again. My friends are peculiar about books. They read all the best-sellers. They go through them as fast as possible. I think they skip a lot. And they NEVER read anything a second time, so they don't remember a word of it a year later. But they are profoundly shocked to see me drop a book in the wastepaper basket or give it away. The way they look at it, you buy a book, you read it, you put it on the shelf, you never open it again for the rest of your life, but YOU DON'T THROW IT OUT! NOT IF IT HAS A HARD COVER ON IT! Why not? I personally can't think of anything less sacrosanct than a bad book or even a mediocre book. (*During the last sentence Helene has dumped the box of books in her hallway and is seated back at her desk. Frank has entered from upstage and sits on the library ladder reading a book*) Trust you and Nora had a fine holiday. Mine was spent in Central Park. I had a month's vacation from Joey, my dear little dentist; he went on his honeymoon. I financed the honeymoon. Did I tell you he told me last spring I had to have all my teeth capped or all my teeth out? I decided to have them capped, as I have got used to having teeth. But the cost is simply astronomical. So Elizabeth will have to ascend the throne without me; teeth are all I am going to see crowned for the next couple of years. I do not intend to stop buying books, however; you have to have something. (*Sound of Westminster Abbey bells. H.H. takes out of her desk drawer a small Union Jack flag which she sticks in a vase on bookshelves*) P.S. I plan to crawl out of bed before dawn on Coronation Day to attend the ceremony by radio; will be thinking of you all. Cheers!

FRANK (*Seated in ladder*): June eleventh, 1953, Dear

Helene, Just a note to let you know that your parcel arrived safely on June first just in time for our Coronation celebrations. We had a number of friends at home to watch TV on the day, and so the ham was most welcome to provide them with something to eat. It was delicious. And we all drank to your health as well as the Queen's. (*Bells out. In the street we can see Megan and Bill—in his waistcoat—with a stepladder. Slowly they begin to take down the bunting. Cecily enters shop and proceeds to dismantle interior display*) It was most kind of you to spend your hard-earned money on us like this, and the rest of the staff join me in saying— *thanks a lot!* (*He says this with a broad American accent, as though a baseball player. He turns and sees Cecily observing him. She exits*)

HELENE (*Moving downstage*): Frankie, you'll DIE when I tell you. Now then, Ellery went off the air and I was shuffling around piling up dentist's bills and feeling pale when I was invited to write an outline for a TV show which dramatizes incidents from the lives of famous people. So I rushed home and did an outline of an incident from-the-life-of-a-famous-person and sent it in and they bought it and I wrote the script and they liked it and they're gonna give me more work in the fall. And whaddya think I dramatized? JOHN DONNE ELOPING WITH THE BOSS'S DAUGHTER, out of Walton's *Lives.* (*Frank looks up at this*) Nobody who watches television has the slightest idea who John Donne was— but thanks to Hemingway *everybody* knows No Man Is an Island. All I had to do was work that in and it was sold! (*Frank shakes his head with amusement, collects briefcase, umbrella, and hat, and goes outside, closing door. We can see him talking with Bill and Megan about a new display, then leaving*) So that's how John Donne made the "Hallmark Hall of Fame" and paid for all the books you ever sent me and five teeth!

(*Cecily enters with small round suitcase, and wool sweater which she places on downstage chair. She leaves a note on Frank's desk*)

CECILY: Helene dear, I'm dashing this off to say you must send *nothing at all* to the shop for Christmas; everything is now off rations and even nylons are available in all the better shops. Please save your money, as the most important thing after your dentist is your trip to England. Only don't come in fifty-four, as I shall be in Iraq with Doug where he is now stationed. Come in fifty-five when we shall be back and you can stay with us. (*She is putting on the wool jacket*) Doug writes that our call may come at any moment, as we are next in line for married quarters. The children and I are hoping to join him before Christmas. He is well and happy on Bahrein Island in the middle of the Persian Gulf (if you've got an atlas) but will return to the RAF base at Habbaniya in Iraq when our quarters are available and we will join him there, all being well. (*She picks up the case. Megan and Bill are now entering the shop*) Write again soon. Best wishes— (*She shakes Bill by hand*) and love— (*She kisses Megan, who breaks away to hide her tears. Cecily moves to door of shop, pauses, and then says*) CECILY!

(*They wave as she goes. Bill goes to work upstage center. Megan exits to put away bunting, then returns to sit at center stage table*)

HELENE (*Rising and moving front of desk with Marks catalog*): DO YOU MEAN TO SIT THERE AND TELL ME YOU'VE BEEN PUBLISHING THESE MAMMOTH CATALOGS ALL THESE YEARS AND THIS IS THE FIRST TIME YOU EVER BOTHERED TO SEND ME ONE? THOU VARLET!!!!! I don't remember which Restoration playwright it was who called everyone a varlet! But I've always wanted to use it in a sentence! As it happens, the only thing which MIGHT interest me is the Catullus; it's not the Loeb Classics but it sounds like it'll do. If you still have it, mail it and I'll send you the six shillings twopence as soon as you translate it; Kay and Brian moved to the suburbs and left me without a translator. (*Sound of New York church bells. From sofa she picks up New York* Times) I shall be obliged if you will send Nora and the girls to church every Sunday for the next month to pray for the continued health and strength of the Messrs. Gilliam, Reese, Snider, Campanella, Robinson, Hodges, Furillo, Podres, Newcombe, and Labine, collectively known as the Brooklyn Dodgers. If they lose this World Series I shall do myself in and then where will you be? (*She throws paper back on sofa and looks at her watch, sees time and realizes she's going to be late. Shuffles scripts into briefcase, and winds scarf round neck*) Have you got de Tocqueville's *Journey to America?* Somebody borrowed mine and never gave it back. Why is it that people who wouldn't dream of stealing anything else think it's perfectly all right to steal books? Regards to Megan— (*Megan looks up*) if she's still there. And what's become of Cecily, is she back from Iraq? (*Sound of siren. She exits*)

(*Frank enters, in winter overcoat, scarf, etc. from street. Wintry lighting. He wheezes, and moves with difficulty. He has been ill and come back to work sooner than he should have. Bill and Megan register his arrival and Megan flashes a silent signal: Go and get him a hot drink*)

FRANK: Dear Helene, I feel very guilty about not writing to you before this, but you can put it down to a dose of flu which kept me away from the shop for a couple of weeks. (*Megan takes his umbrella, and puts his briefcase on table*) About the Catullus, I have sent you an edition which contains the Latin text with a verse translation by Sir Richard Burton, and also a prose translation by Leonard Smithers (*He is removing gloves, stuffs them in pockets. Megan then removes his overcoat and hangs it up. He rubs his hands together and goes to desk, perching on high stool*) printed in large type and all for three dollars seventy-eight. We have no edition of de Tocqueville but will keep looking for one for you. (*Megan is now stage right of him*) Megan is still here but planning to go to South Africa to live; we are all trying to talk her out of it. (*Megan, mock indignant, whips hat off his head and crosses to hatstand with it*) Cecily has left and gone out to the East to join her husband, although he was only to be gone a year . . . (*Bill appears with hot drink in a mug and Megan crosses to take it from him. Bill then returns to his work at the table. Megan waits with the drink*) I shall be only too pleased to root for the Brooklyn Dodgers if you will reciprocate with a few cheers for THE SPURS— (*Megan stares at him pretending not to understand. Frank turns and speaks to her as though deaf*) The Tottenham Hotspur Football Club to the uninitiated!— (*Megan bangs down mug on desk and breaks up to Bill. Frank takes his pill here from small bottle in waistcoat pocket*) who are at present languishing next to the bottom of the League. Nora and all here join me in sending our best wishes for Christmas and the New Year. Sincerely, Frank. (*He puts pill in mouth and takes a sip of water*)

(*Megan is moving slowly downstage toward center table. Helene is picking up a pile of television scripts. Helene enters*)

HELENE: *Will you tell Megan Wells she is out of her cotton-picking mind?* (*Megan taken by surprise, reacts. Frank smiles*) If she's that bored with civilization why doesn't she just move to a Siberian salt mine? (*Megan*

sits upstage end of center table, sorting books) South
Africa . . . I can't even imagine it. But to tell the truth,
I'm afraid of traveling . . . I'm *not* afraid of flying.
That's all right . . . I'm afraid of arriving!! But I have
been socking money away in the savings bank for next
summer. If TV keeps feeding me, then I'm finally coming over.

(*As she types, Helene starts to sing "Over There!" Megan
and Bill pick it up, and Frank whistles the tune. All are
delighted at the news. In rhythm to the music Megan is
picking up books, building a pile up to her chin. She
is standing. Suddenly Helene ceases on "The drums
are . . ." All freeze*)

FRANK: March sixteenth, 1956. Dear Helene, We are still
waiting to hear whether you are finally coming to England this summer. (*Freeze. Waiting. Frank looks
round at them. Then back front. A sense of urgency. All
looking front*) Both the girls are away at school so you
will have your choice of beds at Thirty-seven Oakfield
Court. (*Freeze still held. All wait*)

(*Helene doesn't know what to say*)

HELENE (*Very swiftly*): June first, 1956. Dear Frank,
Brian introduced me to Kenneth Graham's *Wind in the
Willows* and I have to have this. With the Shephard illustrations, please, but DON'T MAIL IT—JUST HOLD IT FOR
ME TILL SEPTEMBER— (*Megan and Bill look at each
other, this is it, she is coming in September! They cry
out. Megan rushes to embrace Frank*) and then mail it
to the new address below. (*H.H. breaks down, crying*)

(*Those in shop are stunned. Frank moves downstage left,
unable to believe it. The others watch him. He goes to
desk. Closes register and puts it inside desk. Then he*

*looks at duck and puts away that also. He is "burying" his
pain and disappointment. He crosses to shop door, steps
outside. Megan and Bill watch anxiously. All this spaced
out over the next lines. Helene rises*)

HELENE: The sky fell on us in this cozy brownstone. We
got eviction notices last month; they're renovating the
building. I decided the time had come to get me a real
apartment with real furniture— (*She places scripts,
books, etc. in a large cardboard box*) and in my right
mind and shaking all over I went round to the con-
struction site of a new building going up over on Second Avenue and signed a lease on a two and a half
(bed-sitter) that isn't even there yet. I am now racing
around buying furniture and bookshelves and wall-to-
wall carpeting with all my England money! (*Frank
closes file here and puts it, then the duck, away*) But all
my life I've been stuck in dilapidated furnished rooms
and cockroachy kitchens and I want to live like a lady
even if it means putting off England till it's paid for.
(*She now starts to move the desk to what will be its
new position. Also desk chair*) Meanwhile, the landlord
thinks we are not moving out fast enough and is en-
couraging us by firing the super, leaving nobody to give
us hot water or take the garbage out, and also by rip-
ping out mailboxes, the hall light fixtures and—as of this
week—the wall between my kitchen and bathroom. All
this and the Dodgers disinteg- (*She picks up the paper
and her handbag. Megan has now gone*) rating before
my very eyes, nobody knows the trouble I see! (*She
exits*)

(*Lights change to autumnal glow. We hear a phrase from
the Negro spiritual "Nobody Knows the Trouble I've
Seen." Bill, at his desk, anxiously watches Frank, but
drops his gaze and goes on working when Frank returns.
Takes out pipe and strikes match*)

FRANK: May third, 195– (*He pauses amazed*) 7. Two of your friends dropped in to see us a few days ago and now I have forgotten their names. Unfortunately they only had time to stop and smoke a cigarette, as they were off again on their travels next morning. (*He shuts door and moves to crate*) We seem to have had more American visitors than ever this year, including hundreds of lawyers who march around with a large card pinned to their clothes stating their hometown and name. (*He lifts crate and carries it to front of desk. Bill sees him, shakes his head, then settles to work*) They all seem to be enjoying their trip so you will have to manage it next year. With all good wishes from us all, Frank. (*Puts pipe in mouth, goes to crate just below desk and stoops, looking for a book. Finds it and stands reading it, one foot on edge of crate*)

(*Helene enters with brightly colored scatter cushions, a potted plant, and Nora's Christmas card. The cushions go on sofa, plant on cupboard, card on her board*)

HELENE: 305 East Seventy-second Street, New York 21, New York. Hey, Frankie, tell Nora to bring her address book up to date. Your Christmas card just got here; she sent it to the old address. In your catalog there's a list of MacDonald Illustrated Classics which includes the *Essays of Elia*. I'd love to have this. If it's reasonable, of course. Nothing's cheap anymore. (*She is now unpacking the box with all her scripts, books, etc.*) It's reasonable. Or "sensibly priced." There's a building going up across the street; the sign over it says "One and two bedroom apartments at Rents That Make Sense." Rents do NOT make sense. And prices do not sit around being reasonable about anything, no matter what it says in the ad—which isn't an ad anymore, it's a commercial. (*She is sorting out books on her shelves*) I go through life watching the English language being raped before

my face. Like Miniver Cheevy I was born too late.
And, like Miniver Cheevy, I cough and call it fate and
go on drinking. Whatever became of Plato's minor dialogues? (*She exits*)

FRANK (*Lowers lid of crate*): Dear Helene, I must apologize for taking so long to answer your last letter but we
have had rather a hectic time. Nora has been in the
hospital for the past several months and I have had my
hands full at home. She is almost fully recovered and
will be coming home in a week or so. (*He sits on the
crate. Bill rises and crosses to table center stage to
check something*) It has been a trying time for us
but, thanks to our National Health Service, it hasn't
cost us a penny. I don't know how to break the bad
news but two days after offering you the Shorter Oxford Dictionary for your friend, a man came in and
bought it when my back was turned. (*He looks at Bill,
who shrugs apologetically. Bill moves to pile of books*)
I have delayed replying to your letter in the hope that
another would come along but no luck yet. I am terri-
bly sorry to disappoint your friend but you can blame it
on me, as I really ought to have reserved it. (*He looks
at Bill, who smiles. There is a pause. Bill moves upstage. Frank rises and moves center stage*) About the
MacDonald Classics, we do get a few from time to time
but have none at the moment. We had several copies of
—Lamb's *Essays of* oh, um *Elia* earlier on but they
were snapped up during the holiday rush. I am off on a
buying trip next week and will look out for one for you.
(*He picks up mug from his desk*) Not forgetting the
Plato. We are all sorry to hear that your television
shows have moved to Hollywood and that one more
summer will bring us every American tourist but the
one we want to see. I can quite understand your refusal
to leave New York for *Southern California!* We have
our fingers crossed for you and hope that some sort of
work will turn up soon. Sincerely, Frank. (*Drinks con-*

tents and then he moves upstage with the mug. Stands by Bill)

(H.H. reenters, and puts on dressing gown—large—a man's)

HELENE: Sir, I write to say I have got work. *(Frank looks up at this. Bill rises, takes mug and exits)* I won it. I won a five-thousand-dollar grant off CBS. It's supposed to support me for a year while I write American history dramatizations. *(Frank turns to listen)* I am starting with a script about New York under seven years of British Occupation and I MARVEL at how I rise above it to address you in a friendly and forgiving fashion, your behavior over here from 1776 to 1783 was simply FILTHY. Is there any such thing as a modern version of the Canterbury Tales? I have these guilts about never having read Chaucer. Love to Nora. Anything she needs just let me know. *(She puts on glasses and settles to read a script)*

(The interior of the shop is now wintry. Frank moves downstage a little)

FRANK: Dear Helene! Thank you very much for your kind offer but there really is nothing we need. We are delighted to hear that you've won a grant and are working again. We are prepared to be broad-minded about your choice of subject matter, but I must tell you that one of the young inmates here confessed that until he read your letter he never knew that England had ever owned the States.

(H.H. reacts to the above. Very softly the music of the slow movement from "On the Town." Outside the shop it is now snowing. Frank sits at worktable upstage. H.H. rises and pours out a gin)

HELENE: Sunday night and a hell of a way to start 1960. I don't know, Frankie. (*Frank feels the cold, blows on his hands. He rises and moves to shop window. Watches snow. Puts on scarf and overcoat. Gets out his pipe and matches. H.H. lifts an enormous book off floor*) Somebody gave me this book for Christmas. It's a Giant Modern Library book. Did you ever see one of those? (*She carries book to desk*) It's less attractively bound than the Proceedings of the New York Assembly and it weighs more. It was given to me by a gent who knows I am fond of John Donne. The title of this book is:

The Complete Poetry
and
Selected Prose
of
JOHN DONNE
and
The Complete Poetry
of
WILLIAM BLAKE?

The question mark is mine. Will you please tell me what those two boys have in common, except they were both English and they both wrote? (*Frank moves upstage center to chair at worktable and leans against chair, pipe in mouth, listening*) I tried reading the Introduction figuring that might explain it. The Introduction is in four parts. Parts One and Two include a professor's (*Music out*) life of Donne mit illustrations from the-author's-works-also-criticism. Part Three begins—and God knows I quote: "When, as a little boy, William Blake saw the prophet Ezekiel under a tree amid a summer field, he was soundly trounced by his mother." I'm with his mother! (*On the laugh, Frank moves downstage center*) I mean, the back of the Lord God or the face of the Virgin Mary, all right—but why the hell should anyone want to see the prophet Ezekiel? I don't like Blake anyway, he swoons too much. It's Donne I'm writing about. I am being driven clean up the wall. Frankie, you have got to help me. (*Frank moves swiftly, sits chair at table by desk. H.H. sits in her swivel chair at desk, legs over the armrest*) Here I was, curled up in my armchair so at peace with the world, with something old and serene on the radio—Corelli or somebody—and this thing on the table. This Giant Modern Library thing. So I thought: "I will read the three standard passages from Sermon XV aloud"—you have to read Donne aloud, it's like a Bach fugue. Would you like to know what I went through in an innocent attempt to read three contiguous uncut passages from Sermon XV aloud? (*Frank strikes match and lights pipe. H.H. rises, and relates following speech to the books in question*) You start with the Giant Modern Library version, you locate Sermon XV, and there they are: Excerpts 1, 2, and 3—only when you get to the end of Excerpt 1, you discover they have deleted Jezebel off it. So you get down Donne's *Sermons*, Selected Passages (Logan Pearsall Smith), where you spend twenty minutes locating Sermon XV, Excerpt 1, because by Logan Pearsall Smith it isn't Sermon XV, Excerpt 1, it's Passage 126, *All Must Die*. Now that you've found it, you find he also deleted Jezebel, so you get down the *Complete Poetry and Selected Prose* (Nonesuch Press), but they didn't happen to select Jezebel either, so you get down the *Oxford Book of English Prose*, where you spend another twenty minutes locating it because in the *Oxford English Prose* it isn't Sermon XV, Excerpt 1, nor yet 126, *All Must Die*, it's Passage 113, *Death the Leveller*. Jezebel is there! and you read it aloud, but when you get to the end you find it doesn't have either Excerpt 2 or 3 so you switch to one of the other three books—provided you had the wit to leave all three open in the right pages, which I didn't! So—break it to me gently: how hard is it going to be to find me John

Donne's Complete Sermons, and how much is it going
to cost? (*Frank makes a face. Midnight begins to
strike. Sound of car hooters and crackers, fireworks ex-
ploding, voices shout out "Happy New Year!" All the
bells of New York begin to ring. Helene picks up the
nearly empty gin bottle*) HAPPY NEW YEAR!!!! . . . I'm
going to bed . . . Yours, H. HanF-F-F-F! (*She exits*)

(*Sound out. Light change. It is spring. Frank softly claps
his hands. Enter Bill in Trilby hat and a smart suit, carrying a rolled-up umbrella. He smiles at Frank, hangs up
hat and umbrella. Bill stands at his table sorting the mail.
He takes out horn-rimmed glasses to do this. His hair is
fuller now—styles are changing*)

FRANK: March fifth, 1960. Dear Helene, I have delayed
   answering your last two letters until I had some good
   news to report. (*He rises*) I have managed to obtain a
   copy of the Bernard Shaw–Ellen Terry correspondence.
   It is not a very attractive edition but it is a good clean
   copy and I thought I'd better send it as this is quite a
   popular book and it might be some time before another
   copy comes along. The price is approximately . . . ?
   Oh, dear . . .
BILL: Two dollars eighty-five!
FRANK: Two dollars eighty-five! And you have a credit
   with us of twenty-five cents. (*He rings bell. Thomas,
   the new assistant, enters brightly. Frank stares at him,
   bemused, then hands him the book and the boy exits.
   Bill follows to check he knows what to do*) I'm afraid
   the complete Donne Sermons can be had only by buying Donne's Complete Works. This runs to more than
   forty volumes and would be very expensive if in good
   condition. (*He leans forward on desk, yawns, removing
   his spectacles. Pipe is in his left hand*) We hope you
   had a good Christmas and New Year in spite of Jezebel
   and the Giant Modern Library. Nora joins me in send-

ing best wishes. Sincerely, Frank. (*He falls asleep during the next speech*)

(*Helene enters with book and letter*)

HELENE: Monsieur de Tocqueville's compliments and he begs to announce his safe arrival in America. I enclose three bucks. It's a beautiful book and you can't even call it secondhand, the pages weren't cut. (*Puts book down on desk and takes paper knife from mug to open letter*) Did I tell you I finally found the perfect page-cutter? It's a pearl-handled fruit knife. My mother left me a dozen of them. I keep one in the pencil cup on my desk. Maybe I go with the wrong kind of people, but I'm just not likely to have twelve guests all sitting round simultaneously eating fruit. (*She has now opened the letter and a check flutters out*) Frank? Frank, you still there? (*Sits with letter*) You won't believe this. I sold a story to *Harper's Magazine*—slaved over it for three weeks and they paid me two hundred dollars for it. (*Lifts letter*) Now they've got me writing the story of my life! They're advancing me fifteen hundred dollars to write it and they figure it shouldn't take me more than six months. I don't mind for myself but the landlord worries. So I can't buy any books, much less travel to London, but back in October somebody introduced me to Louis, the Duke of Saint-Simon, in a miserable abridgement and I tore round to the Society Library and got the real thing. And last night I realized I could not supPORT the notion that when I take it back I will have NO Louis in the house. (*She puts check away, and rises*) I'll settle for any edition you can find that you trust. DO NOT MAIL IT! Just buy it, let me know what it costs and keep it there and I'll buy it from you, one volume at a time. Hope Nora and the girls are fine. And anybody else who knows me. Helene. (*She exits*)

(Frank wakes up, his pipe falls to ground. He wipes rheum from eyes and puts on spectacles. Moves to front of desk and picks up pipe. As though to make up for falling asleep on the job, he moves swiftly—still absentmindedly in his overcoat—to center table for the six volumes of Saint-Simon)

FRANK: Dear Helene, You will be pleased to know that we have a copy of the Memoirs of the Duke de Saint-Simon in stock, six volumes nicely bound and in very good condition. *(He moves upstage with the books)* We are sending them off to you today and they should arrive within a week or two. The amount due on them is approximately eighteen dollars seventy-five but don't worry about paying it all at once. *(He rings bell. Thomas enters. Frank moves stage left holding books. He has forgotten he rang for the boy. Thomas follows him)* Your credit will always be good at Marks and Company. It was very good to hear from you again. We are all well and still hoping to see you in England one of these days. Love from us all, Frank. *(He turns and sees boy who gestures toward books. Frank gives them to him, and boy exits. He sits at table right of desk, checking accounts in ledger)*

HELENE *(Reentering)*: Dear Frankie, Enclosed please God please find a ten-dollar bill. It better get there, not many of those float in here these days but Louis wanted me to get him paid off. I'm having trouble with my bank. Nothing infuriates me like those friendly folksy ads in magazines and on TV. Every bank I ever walked into was about as folksy as a cobra. Frankie, I'm gloomy. I just read a casual description of London by Hazlitt—I had to put the book down, suddenly engulfed in a wave of longing that was like homesickness. I wanted to see London the way old people want to see home before they die. And Oxford. I have to see Trinity College where John Donne, John Henry Newman, and Arthur Quiller-Couch all lived in their various long-gone eras. Whatever I know about writing English, those three men taught me, and before I die I want to stand in their freshmen's rooms and call their names blessed! (*She sits on cushions at the edge of the platform very close to Frank*) I thought of you last night. My editor from *Harper's* was here for dinner. We were going over the story of my life and we came to how I dramatized Landor's *Aesop and Rhodope* for the "Hallmark Hall of Fame." We were going over this anecdote and Gene—my editor—said, "Who is Landor?" and I plunged into an enthusiastic explanation and Gene shook her head and cut it impatiently, "You and your Olde English Books!" You see how it is, Frankie?

FRANK: Ummm?

HELENE: You're the only soul alive who understands me. (*Beatles' "Yesterday" starts here. They both hear the music*) P.S. Gene's Chinese.

(*From outside the shop the music of the Beatles' song "Yesterday" can be heard. Frank looks up, rises, goes to door, opens it. It reminds him of something, the Easter duck! He opens desk, brings it out and starts talking to it directly as he sets it once again on his desk*)

FRANK: Dear Helene! You will be surprised to learn that the two volumes of Virginia Woolf's *Common Reader* . . . (*He is moving to low table downstage right by floats*) . . . are on their way to you. If you want anything else I can probably get it for you with the same efficiency and swiftness. (*He finds the two blue volumes of Virginia Woolf in cardboard box. As he straightens up, he has a twinge. Slowly straightening*) We are all jogging along as usual. My eldest daughter Sheila—twenty-four—suddenly decided she wanted to be a teacher so she threw up her secretarial job two years ago to go to college. She has another year to go, so it looks as though it will be a long time before our children will be able to keep us in luxury. Love from all here—Frank. (*Music out. Frank crosses to crate to find the Chaucer. H.H. is reading the Chaucer. Frank lifts end of crate and rummages inside*) P.S. Some time ago you asked me for a modern version of Chaucer's *Canterbury Tales.* I came across a little volume the other day which I thought you would like. It is not complete by any means but it is quite a cheap book . . . I am sending it along by book post. If this whets your appetite for Chaucer (*He holds book up*) let me know and I will see what I can find.

HELENE: All right, that's enough Chaucer made easy! (*Throws it in bin—bang! Frank drops his copy into crate—bang! and slams lid—bang!*) I'm glad I read it. I liked reading about the nun who ate so dainty she never dripped any grease on herself. I've never been able to make that claim and I use a fork. (*Sits on sofa, picks up gin bottle which is on floor and pours a drink. Frank moves to desk, opens big ledger, makes entries, pipe in hand*) Wasn't anything else that interested me much, it's just stories. . . . Now if Chaucer had kept a diary and told me what it was like to be a little clerk in the palace of Richard II—THAT I'd learn Olde English for. I just threw out a book somebody gave me. It was some slob's version of what it was like to live in the time of Oliver Cromwell—only the slob didn't LIVE in the time of Oliver Cromwell, so how the hell does he know what it was like? Anybody wants to know what it was like to live in the time of Oliver Cromwell can flop on the sofa with Milton on his pro side and Walton on his con, and they'll not tell him what it was like, they'll take him there. "The reader will not credit that such things could be," Walton says somewhere or other, "but I was there and I saw it." (*She picks up bottle, glass, and a book from desk, is about to go on working*) That's for me. I'm a great lover of I-was-there books. (*Bill enters*)

I enclose two bucks for the Virginia Woolf and that leaves me with a credit with you of sixty-five cents, which is a larger credit than I have anywhere else. (*Bill rings bell*) Do you ever hear anything of Cecily or Megan?

(*Enter Mrs. Todd. Bill talks to her. Tom follows with trolley and starts to clear books. He exits with a load. Frank is still in his overcoat and scarf. Bill crosses to him with the post, which includes a quilted envelope enclosing the E. M. Delafield*)

FRANK: Dear Helene, It was good to hear from you again. We have not heard from Cecily Farr in some years now. Megan Wells had enough of South Africa in a very short time and did stop in to give us a chance to say I-told-you-so before going out to try her luck in Australia. We had a Christmas card from her a few years ago but nothing recently. (*Sorting the mail, he finds package and opens it*) I've just managed to obtain a copy of E. M. Delafield's *Diary of a Provincial Lady* and am sending it off to you today. (*He holds out book. Mrs. Todd takes it from him and rings bell for Tom, who reenters. Frank moves downstage center*) We had a very pleasant summer with more than the usual number of tourists, including hordes of young people making the pilgrimage to CARNABY STREET. (*Bill checks his watch: time for his lunch break. Closes his file and crosses to get hat and umbrella*) We watch it all from a safe distance, though I must say I rather like the Beatles. (*Bill is at door and he and Frank exchange smile on next line. Mrs. Todd and Thomas also smile*) If their fans just wouldn't scream so! Yes, we're still here, getting older and busier, but no richer. (*Bill exits. Also Mrs. Todd and Thomas*) Nora and the girls send their love. Frank. (*He moves down to crate to fill up with books that are on floor. The crate has a false bottom, so it will be only half full when he lifts it*)

(*Helene enters in long housecoat which conceals her final costume. Her hair is grayer*)

HELENE: September thirtieth, 19—68! Still alive, are we? (*She picks up cardboard box and starts to pack text-books. Frank is on his knees downstage also packing books*) I've been writing American history books for children for four or five years. (*Frank moving down-stage to crate here*) Got hung up on the stuff and have been buying American history books—in ugly cardboardy American editions, but somehow I just didn't think the stately homes of England would yield nice English editions of James Madison's stenographic record of the Constitutional Convention or T. Jefferson's letters to J. Adams or like that. Are you a grandfather yet? (*Frank, pipe in mouth, looks up*) Tell Sheila and Mary their children are entitled to presentation copies of my *Collected Juvenile Works* . . . THAT should make them rush off and reproduce. (*He smiles. She lifts cardboard box*) I introduced a young friend of mine to *Pride and Prejudice* one rainy Sunday and she has gone out of her mind for Jane Austen. She has a birthday around Halloween, can you find me some Austen for her? If you've got a complete set let me know the price; if it's expensive, I'll make her husband give her half and I'll give her half. Best to Nora and everybody else round, Helene. (*She carries box to her hall, then re-turns to desk, sips gin, picks up the Newman, caresses it, then returns to her notes*)

(*During next speech, Frank closes lid of crate, lifts it— very heavy—and carries it toward center stage, but has to drop it on floor. It is snowing once again outside the shop*)

FRANK: Dear Helene, Yes we are all very much alive and kicking, though rather exhausted from a hectic summer with hordes of tourists from the U.S.A., France, Scandinavia, etc., all buying our nice leather-bound books. Consequently our stock at the moment is a sorry sight, and with the shortage of books and high prices there is little hope of finding any Jane Austen for you in time for your friend's birthday. Perhaps we will be able to find them for her for Christmas. (*Lowers crate. Bent over. Slowly straightens. Pause. Shakes himself. Leaves crate. He has decided to go home. Will collect hat, case, and umbrella*) Nora and the girls are fine. Sheila is teaching. Mary is engaged to a very nice boy, but there is little hope of them getting married for some time as neither has any money! So Nora's hopes of being a glamorous grandmother are receding fast. (*Door opens, he looks round shop*) Love, Frank. (*He exits*)

(*Enter from outer office, briskly, Mrs. Todd, with file. She crosses to Frank's desk, and puts duck inside*)

JOAN TODD: Dear Miss Hanff . . . (*Helene looks up*) I have just come across the letter you wrote to Mr. Doel on the thirtieth of September last, and it is with great regret that I have to tell you that he passed away on Sunday the twenty-second of December. The funeral took place last week. He was rushed to the hospital and operated on at once for a ruptured appendix. Unfortunately peritonitis set in and he died seven days later.

(*On the last three words she slowly closes ledger and exits, then upstage center as lights on shop fade to black, leaving only Helene, who continues the letter, as though knowing it by heart*)

HELENE: He had been with the firm for over forty years and naturally it has come as a very great shock to Mr.

Cohen, particularly coming so soon after the death of Mr. Marks. He is left with no alternative but to close the shop . . . Yours faithfully, Joan Todd—for Marks and Company.

(*In the darkened shop, the shelves in windows swivel and become filled with copies of the book* 84 Charing Cross Road. *Sound of jet plane. Lights fade on Helene who is in tears. In the blackout she exits to change, and under cover of the plane noise the bookshelves in the shop are slid away, revealing empty shelves when lights come up. The Pilot's announcement covers this—giving the actress time also to get round to the other side of stage. Once the shelves are clear, lights come up slowly on shop. In practice it should be a cross fade from one area to another. If there is a total blackout, the audience is likely to applaud, assuming it is the end*)

PILOT: Ladies and gentlemen, this is the Captain speaking. We will be landing at Heathrow Airport in approximately ten minutes. Would you kindly fasten your seatbelts, bring your seats to the upright positions, and observe the no-smoking signs. We hope that you enjoyed your flight and that you will fly with us again. Thank you.

(*Plane heard disappearing into distance. Silence—no music here, that is important. We see Helene in a blue trouser suit, blue handbag over shoulder, red-white-blue scarf knotted around neck, and holding a copy of her book. In "The Duchess of Bloomsbury" we read how the empty bookshop was stuffed with copies for the press launching. She opens door, gazes inside, enters, moves slowly into center of shop. Removes her glasses and only then speaks*)

HELENE: Theoretically it was one of the happiest days of my life. Year after year I'd planned a pilgrimage only to have it canceled at the last minute by some crisis, usually financial. This time it was different. I'd written a book called 84 *Charing Cross Road* (*She gazes at the reality again*) and a few months after it came out in New York in 1971, a London publisher, named Andre Deutsch, bought it for publication in England. He wrote me that the London edition would be brought out in June and he wanted me there to help publicize the book. (*She moves toward Frank's desk*) It had felt unreal knowing I was on my way to that address. I'd bought books from here for twenty years. I'd made friends here whom I never met. Most of the books I bought from Marks and Company were probably available in New York, but I'd wanted a link with London and I'd managed it. (*She has put down her book*) How about this, Frankie? I finally made it.

(*Music of* London Suite—Knightsbridge—*starts softly and builds and will play fortissimo through the curtain calls. Helene's hand moves out to caress the ledger*)

THE END